THE GRAND LOUVRE

CONTENTS

Cover:
The Pyramide and
the Denon Wing.
© L. Boegly/
Archipress.

Opposite: The Salle
des Caryatides, Denon
Wing.

THE LOUVRE, A CHEQUERED HISTORY

The history of the Louvre is long and complex, reflecting that of the French nation. For some eight centuries, plans were drawn up and buildings built, often to be revamped or torn down. By turns the residence of the kings of France, a seat of revolutionary power, a place for public festivities and a prison, the Louvre finally became a museum. It is an amalgam of architectural styles, including Renaissance buildings as well as a handsome classical 17th-century colonnade.

The Louvre was originally not a palace but a fortification, built north of Paris by King Philippe Auguste (1165-1223). At the time, the capital was divided into two main quarters, the Ile de la Cité on the Seine and the University on the Left Bank. But the city was expanding rapidly and had to be protected on the Right Bank at a spot known as "Lupara", (which over time was transformed into "Louvre"). Moats were dug, and high walls and watchtowers raised. Vestiges of these fortifications can be seen today under the courtyard known as the Cour Carrée, and especially at the base of what was once a nearly 100-foot-high donjon where the royal archives, furniture and the Crown treasure were originally kept.

Philippe Auguste's fortification marked the city limits on the Right Bank and symbolized the King's desire to expand his domain. From that time on, the construction of the Louvre corresponded roughly to a consolidation of the French kings' power. Louis IX, known as Saint Louis, had the great hall of the castle installed in the 12th century. Dating from the same period is the crypt of Saint Louis, where the archeological discoveries made during the recent excavations are now on view. Around 1360, Charles V had his architect Raymond du Temple enlarge and revamp the existing buildings. Among other things, he had his library

Left, view of the donjon created by Philippe Auguste. Right, miniature, "Les Très Riches Heures of the Duc de Berry", by the Limbourg brothers. Chantilly, Musée Condé.

The impressive stone foundations of the Louvre's Mediaeval fortress, now on view to the public, allows us today to imagine what it was like in Philippe Auguste's fortified chateau. Symbol of the strengthening of royal power, this defence machine, a back-up to the Paris ramparts, was hardly a comfortable place to reside. Anyway, the King preferred his Cité palace. In the 14th century, when Charles V finally decided to take up residence in the Louvre, he had major improvements made, of which the famous miniature "Les Très Riches Heures of the Duc de Berry" is a reminder.

Merry-Joseph Blondel, The Making of Chambres by Louis XIII, former room of the State Council.
Below, Anonymous, *A Ball at the Court of Henri III*, around 1851.

installed in one of the towers. It was from this time on that the Louvre became a royal residence, even though the palace on the Ile de la Cité was still the official residence.

The kingdom was still quite fragile. During the Hundred Years War, which pitted France against England, all work on the Louvre came to a halt as the English occupied Paris. Henry V, who had been proclaimed King of France illegally, took up residence in the Louvre, as did the Duke of Bedford after him. The French kings who followed, turned their back on Paris to live in their châteaux on the Loire. The Louvre was turned into an ammunition depot and housed certain royal administrations. When the kings deigned to stay in Paris, they preferred the Hôtel de Tournelles, which they found less austere than the Louvre, still an uncomfortable medieval castle. It was François I (1494-1547) who was to turn the Louvre into a palace fit for a king.

As the kingdom was now secure, François I felt there was no longer any need for such massive defenses, nor did he need the Louvre to be a symbol of feudal power, for his own authority was firmly established. He therefore decided that the "big tower" (the donjon of Philippe Auguste) was to be torn down and the moats filled (the same moats that were recently excavated to reveal the base of the donjon).

François I had called upon Italian artists and architects for his new châteaux. But this was going to be the first major realization of Renaissance art in Paris. For it, he named the French architect Pierre Lescot to build an Italianate palace worthy of so great a patron of the arts and chose the great French sculptor Jean Goujon to decorate it. The royal apartments were designed so as to give onto the

The Hundred Years War and the construction of new royal residences in the Loire valley, served to keep the Court away from the Louvre chateau for many a year. However, in 1528, François Ist decided to transform this fortress into a sumptuous palace in the new Italian style. The Mediaeval donjon was destroyed to make room for delicately sculptured Renaissance columns and pediments in coloured marble. An anonymous 16th century painting recreates for us the atmosphere of a royal entertainment at the Louvre under Henri III.

river, which meant that the medieval towers on the Seine had to be torn down as well.

The results of Lescot's work were impressive: the façade of the Louvre now had a classical ordonnance, with larger windows. Numerous apartments were installed to accomodate a growing court of noblemen dependent upon the king. When the Holy Roman Emperor Charles V came on a state vist in 1540, he was duly impressed: he found a spanking new palace with the royal coat of arms proudly displayed on the facade, and grandly decked out for the occasion.

Lescot continued this mammoth undertaking after the demise of François I. Under Henri II, the western part of the palace was revamped and the vast Cour Carrée was created. For a short time the Louvre was the only royal residence in Paris. Then Henri's widow, the famous Catherine de Medicis, chose to erect a new palace to the West of the city, just outside the old medieval walls. It was on the site of a tile manufacture, hence the name "Les Tuileries". It was comprised of a central pavilion topped by a dome and flanked by two buildings ending in a pavilion. It was not long before the idea cropped up of building a gallery to link the Louvre to the Tuileries Palace.

The "Grande Galerie" running along the Seine was completed under the reign of Henri IV (1589-1610), who planned to build a similar one on the north side. (His "grand design" was taken up by succeeding sovereigns, but was completed only in the 1860s.)

When Henri IV was assassinated in 1610, his body was transported to the Grande Galerie. With such tragic memories attached to the place, his widow Marie de Medicis decided to build herself a new palace on the Left Bank, the Palais du Luxembourg, which now houses the French Senate. Her son, Louis XIII, was not particularly attracted by the Louvre, but nonetheless continued the work begun by Lescot. He entrusted the architect Lemercier with the task of building a second wing, to match that of François I. It was to be the Pavillon de l'Horloge (Clock Pavilion), otherwise known as the Pavillon de Sully, with its imposing curved roof that became the latest fahion in architecture. (His widow, in turn, preferred to live in the nearby Palais Cardinal, donated to the Crown by the King's most powerful minister Cardinal Richelieu and rebaptised Palais Royal.)

During the terrible seven-year civil war called La Fronde, Louis XIV was still a boy, and his mother, the Regent, took refuge once again in the Louvre. With Louis XIV on the throne, an international competition was launched to find new ideas for the Louvre. Among the Italian architects consulted was Bernini, then at the height of his fame, who was treated royally upon his arrival in Paris. And though he laid the foundation stone for a new façade before returning to Rome in October 1665, his project was never to see the light of day. Instead of Bernini's Baroque creation, Louis XIV preferred the classical Colonnade of the French architect Claude Perrault to face onto the church of Saint-Germain-l'Auxerrois.

But the Sun King had a much more ambitious scheme, to wit, a new palace at Versailles. In 1678 he moved his court, along with his government, to the new city. Henceforth the King lost all interest in the Louvre: the gardens that had been redesigned by Le Nôtre were left unfinished, and a number of buildings were not even roofed over.

Part of the palace was then turned into royal storehouses, while the rest became office space for, among others, the French Academy and the

Painting and Sculpture *Academy.* In 1699, the Academy of Science even took over the King's apartments. Artists set up their studios in the Grande Galerie, and by the 18th century, a painter like François Boucher could prevail upon Madame de Pompadour to obtain an apartment in the Louvre. The painters and sculptors were soon joined by courtiers, among others, who gradually took over the entire palace. Everyone did as they pleased, knocking out walls and ceilings. The place was in such a state of disrepair that Louis XV finally charged first Gabriel and then Soufflot with the task of renovating the palace and clearing the Colonnade of the shacks that had cropped up in front of it. Though war brought renovation work to a halt, the idea slowly began to develop of using the Louvre to show the masterpieces belonging to the Crown, which were until then scattered around the various royal residences.

In 1776 the Grande Galerie officially became the « Muséum Français » but before the museum was ready to be opened to the public, the Revolution broke out. It was not until November 18, 1793, that Parisians were able for the first time to cross the threshold of what had been the home of their Kings. As the armies of first the Revolution and then the Napoleonic Empire drained Europe of its treasures, thousands of new works of art were added to the art collections begun by François I and considerably augmented by Louis XIV.

Then Napoleon went a step further to build up the museum: he evicted all the artists and other undesirable occupants and asked architects Percier and Fontaine to link the Louvre to the Tuileries. But he succeeded no better than his predecessors, though he did manage to begin work on the North wing along the Rue de Rivoli and had the pink and grey Arc de Triomphe at the Carrousel built.

Upon Napoleon's defeat at Waterloo 1815, the allied powers of Europe demanded that their works of art be returned. The years that followed were not particularly noteworthy for the Louvre, though it was under Louis XVIII that the Venus de Milo entered the museum.

At long last, Napoleon III (1808-1873) succeeded in linking the Louvre to the Tuileries. The architect Visconti, and then Lefuel, were to carry out the grand design. But first the slum between the two palaces had to be cleared before construction could start. Work on the North wing was begun again, and two enormous pavilions copied from the Louvre of Lescot and Lemercier rose up. All in vain! On May 23, 1871, during the uprising of the Commune, the Tuileries was set on fire, and nothing remained but a charred stone carcass.

The two arms of stone that were to have stretched out to embrace the Tuileries now gave onto the void. The government of the Third Republic decided to clear the rubble and to open up a magnificent vista to the Arc de Triomphe, a vista that has enchanted visitors to the city for over a century.

The decision to turn the Louvre into "the world's biggest museum" was taken in the autumn of 1981 by the then recently elected French President François Mitterrand. The project was indeed ambitious. The challenge lay in turning what was basically a 19th-century museum into a modern museum equipped to handle the ever-growing number of people anxious to see and learn about art. The first step towards creating the "Grand Louvre", as the project came to be called, was to create more exhibition space and to reorganize the collections, so that works could be presented both more logically and with more breathing space. The Louvre also needed more infrastructure to carry out its tasks. The most obvious way to create more exhibition

The Grande Galerie, adorned with masterpieces from the four corners of Europe, witnesses the passing of the wedding cortege of Napoleon and Marie-Louise. Inspite of the monarchy's abandonment of the Louvre since 1647, the palace did not lose any of its political function.
Benjamin Zix, *The Wedding of Napoleon and Marie-Louise,* 1810.

A picture of devastation, the Tuileries palace is reduced to a pile of rubble after the fire of 1871. George Clairin, *The Tuileries Fire*, 1871.

space was to schedule the departure of the Ministry of Finance, which occupied the Richelieu wing of the palace that gives onto the Rue de Rivoli.

In 1981, a few months after his election to the French presidency, François Mitterand outlined a new grand design for the Louvre. "I have decided, without wishing to offend anyone, to return the Louvre to its intended purpose." With these words which sealed his decision to have the Finance Ministry leave the "rue de Rivoli", that is to say the north wing – the so-called Richelieu wing which it had occupied since 1871, the president gave the go-ahead for what was to become a huge building site. The aim of the "Grand Louvre" project is to transform the illustrious Parisian museum into a great modern museum, the biggest in the world, with its collections entirely rearranged before 1997, owing to a doubling of the exhibition space (it will increase from 31,000 m^2 to more than 60,000 m^2), and from now on in possession of all necessary scientific, cultural and technical equipment for the conservation of the exhibits and for the reception of an ever more demanding public.

The rebalancing of the museum eastwards entailed a complete rethink of all the access and circulation ways. As a consequence of this the American architect of Chinese origin, Ieoh Ming Pei, appointed by the French President in March 1983, proposed developing the understructure of the Cour Napoleon, long thought of as the most rational solution. His project of raising a glass pyramid of more than 20 metres in height, in the centre of the Cour Napoléon, was the subject of lively controversy by virtue of its "modernist" aspect. As a pure form, eminently symbolic, reminiscent of ancient architecture, and yet with a complex geometric structure, the pyramid asserts itself above all by its "absence of style", explains Ieoh Ming Pei, who is assisted by the associated architects Macary and Duval. As it is, the pyramid, with the three pyramidia and the seven triangular basins in dark granite which surround it form a very neutral mineral grouping which barely disturbs the

classical arrangement of the façades of the palace. Inaugurated on 30 March 1989, the Pyramid disclosed its rather more genial underpinnings. Designed as the monumental entrance to the museum, it bathes in light the huge Napoleon Hall, furbished with light-coloured stone and concrete, which sees the daily jostle-free interweaving of thousands of visitors. In addition to the pyramid, which was the focus of attention at the time, this first stage of work also dealt with the setting up of reception and temporary exhibition areas as well as creating access to the spectacular foundations of the medieval Louvre that had been uncovered during the excavations beneath the Cour Carrée. It also included the opening of the first newly refitted rooms: the Caryatid room, the Manège room, twelve rooms of French paintings (from the 15th to the end of the 18th century).

In December 1992 it was the turn of the 39 other rooms of French paintings to reveal their new displays high up in the Cour Carré.

It was however necessary to wait until 1993, the bicentenary year of the museum's foundation, in order to discover the principal stage of the "Grand Louvre" project with the opening of the Richelieu wing. From this part of the palace, built between 1852 and 1857 by Visconti and Lefuel, only the façades and the historical parts (the sumptuous Napoleon III appartments and the monumntal staircases) have been preserved. The architects Ieoh Ming Pei, Michel Macary and Jean-Michel Wilmotte have replaced the six floors of offices vacated by the Finance Ministry with three levels of exhibition rooms fitting in with the rythm of the palace façades. The three interior courtyards which had served as parking areas, have been converted into superb glass-roofed spaces for large-scale French sculpture (Marly and Puget courtyards) and the exceptional group of Assyrian sculptures from the Khorsabad site (Khorsabad courtyard). Owing to the 21,500 square metres made available in

Left page:
the Pyramid and the Richelieu pavilion.
Opposite:
the Puget wing with, in the foreground, a sculpture by Bosio: *Hercules fighting the river god Acheloüs metamorphosed into a serpent*, Richelieu wing.

this way, the collections of objets d'art, French sculpture, Northern Schools paintings, French paintings, oriental antiquities and the Islamic section at last attain suitable dimensions. A quarter of the 12,000 items displayed in the 165 rooms and three courtyards have come out of the reserves, which is a measure of the revelations.

The effect of discovery is also related to the new display conditions of the exhibits. Though the interior decoration of the rooms is deliberately sobre, their volume has been designed to relate to the exhibits within them. The dimensions of the Rubens Gallery, for example, have been specially studied to receive the group of 24 canvases of Rubens' allegorical cycle painted for the Palais du Luxembourg.

Particular care has been taken everywhere with the lighting, be it overhead lighting or lighting for display cabinets where the most sophisticated technology has been used (fibre optics).

The originality and charm of this new Louvre is also to be seen in the choice of strong colours – blues or greens – for certain hangings which creates an atmosphere of sumptuous warmth.

Fourteen years of exceptionally wide-ranging work will have brought about a complete redistribution of the collections, guided by a desire for greater coherence of the itinerary for visitors and an adaptation of the space to the imperatives of exhibition.

The saga of the Grand Louvre is written with superlatives: 6 hectares of land have been dug by archeologists, 11 hectares of façades and 7 of roofing have been renovated, thousands of works of art have been restored and cleaned, the reception areas for the public have been multiplied by ten... The Louvre has become the Louvre-City which hums with the activity of its 1500 employees and the toing and froing within its walls of five million visitors a year.

Jérôme Coignard, Joël Girard, Christophe Lagrange

THE COLLECTIONS

Wished for by a King, created by the nation in revolution, and organised by the State, the Louvre Museum, besides its preeminence and the richness of its collections, is exceptional because it is the only one in the world to link a monarch's collection, witness to France's royal past, to a variety of collections resulting from purchases or gifts. So, far from being frozen in time with the splendours of royal treasures, the Louvre was able to revitalize itself, opening itself up to new horizons and new perspectives on art history and archeology.

Collecting works of art was in olden times a royal activity. The King liked to surround himself with anything that would enhance the brilliance of his reign. He demonstrated his family's prestige by amassing treasures handed down from generation to generation. The first French collector-King was Francois 1st. His collection, built on the inheritance of a few Italian paintings left by Louis XII, brought together paintings, sculptures, and reproductions, all strongly Italianist in style. His paintings, thirty nine in total according to Del Pozzo, including the Mona Lisa and several star works in the current museum, were blended into the decor of the Appartement des Bains in the chateau de Fontainebleau. After Francois 1st we have to wait until Louis XIV to find a King interested in his collections. He bought Cardinal Mazarin's collections one by one, then those of the banker Jabach, in which amongst other masterpieces were Titian's *Entombment* and *Concert in the Country*. Colbert, who advised his King on the purchase of the collections, also suggested his making them accessible to connaisseurs. This advice was ignored by Louis XIV, who took his works of art with him to Versailles. The inventory of the Crown's collections, carried out in 1683 by Le Brun, listed 2,000 paintings.

Louis XV and Louis XVI were not exactly collectors, but in their desire to uphold the great tradition of French art by commissioning works from artists, they accelerated the need for their collections to be made public. The 18th century saw a real popularisation of art appreciation: the number of collectors increased, and in the wake of the bi-annual exhibitions organised by the Academy in the Salon carré of the Louvre, a whole debate on artistic matters sprang up. In the mid-18th century this debate centered around the deterioration of French art, corrupted by bad example. It was then, in 1749, that a solution to this problem was formulated. This would be the creation of a museum, as advocated by Lafont de Saint-Yenne, who said that "A superior means of safeguarding our school from its current propensity towards ruin, and one worthy of the greatness and magnificence of our King, would be the construction of a large gallery, or several well lit adjoining ones, in the chateau du Louvre". This association of museum/Louvre was soon taken up, and first led Louis XV, then Louis XVI, to envisage the creation of this museum. But in spite of the efforts of the Marquis d'Angvillers, placed in charge of the transformation of the Louvre's Great Gallery into the Royal Museum of the Arts, it was the Revolution that was to make the royal collections "humanity's universal heritage".

Caught between the desire to destroy anything that remotely evoked the Ancien Régime, works of art included, and that of preserving the image of man's creative genius, the Convention chose in 1792 to create the Central Museum of the Arts. It opened for the first time on the 10th August 1793, bringing together, besides the royal collections, works seized from the clergy and emigrés, in the Louvre palace. By reinstituting one of the monarch's duties, which was to protect the arts and artists, and by creating this museum, the Convention was making a highly political statement. The museum was in fact considered "one of the most powerful ways of illustrating the French Republic", and "its creation must be strongly upheld by the firm will of the nation so that the capital of injustice, renewed by its freedom, becomes the capital of the arts". Such a position justified, even before it was artic-

ulated, taking spoils of war. Thousands of works lifted from the countries conquered by the revolutionary armies were to flood the museum from 1794 onwards. These works, from Belgium, Holland, but particularly from Italy, radically altered the face of the museum. Under the Directoire and the Consulate, it was a real political instrument to the glory of the army. It also became the site for the Museum of Antiquities inaugurated in 1800, the reflection of the neoclassical aesthetic ideal, advocated since Winckelmann, and serving as a permanent recognition of the power of the Roman Republic.

Stripped, at the fall of the Empire, of all the treasures it had taken from abroad (with the exception of a few works like Veronese's *The Wedding Feast at Cana*), the Louvre continued as before to enhance its collections, profiting, amongst other things, from the interest in the study of ancient civilisations that it had helped awaken in its first visitors. Because experts saw evidence of vanished civilisations through art, the Louvre had a justification for increasing its collections and its scope. The three antiquity departments benefited the most from this phenomenon. Moreover, the setting up of two of them was directly linked to scientific research: the Department of Egyptian Antiquities (in 1826), and the Department of Oriental Antiquities created under this name in 1881 (even though an Assyrian Museum, was in existence since 1847). A large part of these department's collections come from onsite excavations, due to equal share agreements drawn up with the countries concerned.

The museum has continued to hold its political function during its history – the sovereign Heads of State lived close by in the Tuileries palace up until 1870 and used certain of its rooms for official ceremonies, the 1848 rebels wanted to burn it down, it was renamed at every change of regime, and more recently in 1981, Francois Mitterrand decided by himself on the construction of his pyramid – but it has nevertheless developed little by little into a real

Left; Hubert Robert,
The Grande Galerie,
about 1795.
Anonymous, *The
Museum of
Antiquities*,
beginning of the
19th century.

Left; Louis Beroud, *The Rubens Room* in the Louvre, 1904. Below; Francois-Joseph Heim, *Charles X, Distributing Award to the Artists at the End of the Salon*, 1827. Right; Giuseppe Gastiglione, *The Salon Carre*, 1861.

institution. Each government has had at heart the desire to make the old royal palace into a proper museum, undertaking different alteration projects, which are in themselves evidence of the changing nature of styles and museum presentation. Architects have come and gone, each trying to harmonise form and content, and to introduce a certain coherence in this disparate museum, dispersed around the four corners of the palace. The style of presentation was also constantly evolving, the seven departments gradually taking on the appearance we know them for today. Important acquisitions have contributed to this reshaping and to the chronological presentation of the different sections. Thus the purchase by Napoleon of the Campana Gallery (1861) allowed both the exposition of 14th and 15th century Italian painting, highly neglected up until then, and also the showing of Greek ceramic art side by side with major antique sculptures.

Often freer and more adventurous, private collectors have brought to the Louvre, through bequests or donations, major works that the museum or the State might well have let escape. What would the Louvre be without the complete collections given or bequeathed by La Caze in 1865? In 1988 the exhibition *Donators to the Louvre* listed in total more than 2,700 donators. The first gift, from Bertrand Clauzel in 1798 (Gerard Dou's *The Dropsical Woman*), was unanimously greeted as "a patriotic gesture". Other donators have felt they were "carrying out a public service". Whatever the personal reasons for a donation, it should be noted that very early on the Louvre was lodged in people's minds as universal property that behove everyone to held build up. An awareness perpetuated today when each visitor pays their entrance fee, thus buying into the scheme to put the finishing touches to the work in progress since the 16th century, namely the formation of the largest museum in the world. **Laurence Madeline.**

Abandoned by the monarchy who resided in the Tuileries, the Louvre remains at the centre of aristic life throughout the 19th century. It was in the Museum's Salon carré that traditionally the "Salon" was organised (hence its name), which was to remain for decades the most important presentation of contemporary art. To exhibit in the salon was for the artist the only means of making contact with the public, attracting the attention of critics and collectors, and, best of all, making a sale or getting a commission from the State. At the end of the Salon the distribution of awards placed the artists on the road to success.

NEAR EASTERN ANTIQUITIES

The discoveries unearthed during Napoleon's campaign in Egypt created a revolution in archeology and completely overturned established beliefs. In 1824, when Champollion finished deciphering the Egyptian hieroglyphs—which had remained incomprehensible for several thousand years—the West abandoned mythical and aesthetic ideas of Antiquity and entered a period of positive understanding. For Europeans, this discovery of a long-forgotten history put an end to the monopoly of the Greek and Roman cultures as the origins of their civilizations. Archeologists then expanded their research to the Middle East.

Excavations by French archeologist Paul Emile Botta at Khorsabad brought to light the ruins of the palace built by King Sargon of Assyria. The fabulous gates depicting winged bulls with human heads traveled down the Tigres River on specially built rafts, then navigated around Africa and Cape Horn, finally arriving in Marseille. They were then transported overland to Paris. In 1847 an Assyrian museum was inaugurated in the Louvre. It joined the Egyptian, Greek and Roman collections that had been placed in rooms of the former royal residence. The increasing number of treasures from Mesopotamia, Iran, Anatolia, Levant, Cyprus and Carthage resulted in the creation of a Department of Near Eastern Antiquities; in 1890 an Islamic art section was added. These various collections continued to grow throughout the twentieth century.

Today, the Department of Near Eastern Antiquities includes objects spanning more than 8,000 thousand years of history and a geographical area extending from India to North Africa. The most impressive collections come from the fertile crescent, which, from southern Iran to the Mediterranean Sea, formed Mesopotamia. These are the regions where mankind emerged from the shadows of prehistory with the development of metal-working, the discovery of the wheel, the first cities, the calculation of time through astronomical measurements and the invention of writing. Since the autumn of 1997, 7,000 objects from these collections are displayed in eleven renovated rooms that occupy nearly 4,000 square meters of the Sully Wing. The works range from tiny objects, such as a woman at prayer, sculpted in alabaster in Susa some 5,000 years ago, or the black statuette of the Sumerian Prince Gudea, whose diorite robe is covered with cabalistic signs, to monumental works, including a capital of a column from the Apadana,or audience hall, in the palace of Persian King Xerxes, excavated by Dieulafoy in 1884. The Islamic collection has been housed in thirteen rooms of the Richelieu Wing since 1993.

With cultures so diverse—from the banks of the Indus River to the Phoenicians at Carthage, the Hittites of Anatolia, Arabia, antique Lagash and the Ottomans—an obvious question is raised: Why are they all grouped in a single Department, as opposed to the collections of ancient Egypt and classical Greece? It was a valid decision. In addition to the fact that these works were the last antiquities to be discovered, and were unearthed almost simultaneously by European archaeologists, the linguistic relationships and the economic and geopolitical interdependence, and technological and cultural exchanges throughout an extremely long history fully justify such an organization.

The Louvre is a treasure-trove of antique art. And finally, after fifteen years of major renovations, which will be complete in 1998, it will have a new look. At the dawn of the third millennium, the majestic museum created two hundred years ago continues its vocation as a guardian of the memory of mankind, combining science and art to meet our constantly growing need for knowledge and unquenched desire for treasure.

Jules Merleau-Ponty

*Prince Gudea
of Lagash left behind
a large number
of statues, all in
stone, showing
him at prayer.*
Gudea with Vase,
Lagash, ca. 2150
B.C., calcite.

*Found in the temple
of Ishtar, goddess
of love and fertility,
the statue of the
administrator Ebih-Il,
clothed in a goat's
skin, demonstrates
the smiling realism
of Sumerian art.*
Administrator Ebih-Il,
Mari, ca. 2400 B.C.,
alabaster and
lapis-lazuli.

MESOPOTAMIA

While each of the Near Eastern civilizations had a separate approach to art, they nevertheless influenced each other. The Mesopotamian art in the Louvre encompasses several styles that correspond to different periods. Sumerian art is essentially religious, as in the statues discovered at Mari; they are ex-votos, idealized portraits of figures at prayer. The same is true of the neo-Sumerian period, with effigies of Gudea. Unlike Egyptian art, there was no set of artistic criteria, yet the artists tried to achieve the same perfection. Art was also used for funerary purposes, as in the necropolis at Ur, and for royal propaganda—testified by the Code of Hammurabi from the Babylonian period. These principles were shared by all Near Eastern civilizations. In Mesopotamia, stone was used for objects meant to last throughout time, while earthenware was the material of choice for everyday purposes.
Alain Charron

Hammurabi, king of Babylonia, is portrayed standing before Samash, the sun god and protector of justice, on this code of laws. Code of Hammurabi, Susa, ca. 1750 B.C., diorite.

Sumerians invented the earliest form of writing, known as cuneiform (from the Latin "cuneus"), by stamping wedges into wet clay. Tablet with numerical information, Tello, ca. 3000 B.C., baked clay.

The monumental
bull capitals
in the "apadana",
or audience hall,
sit atop columns
20 meters high
and reflect the
magnificence of
monumental Near
Eastern architecture.
Bull capitals, Palace
of Darius I, Susa,
ca. 500 B.C.,
limestone.

The seals used to
identify traded goods
often included
figurative sequences
formed by the
cylindrical shapes.
Cylinder seal
and its imprint,
a woman greeting
a figure before an
altar, Achaemenid
and Persian period,
chalcedony.

IRAN

Bordered by the high mountains of Zagros and Elburz between Mesopotamia and central Asia, the vast plains of ancient Iran were home to a multitude of cultures, which intermingled over the centuries. The region of Elam, whose capital was Susa, was at the center of these exchanges. It was inhabited as early as the 4th millennium B.C., and precious vestiges of a kingdom formed by the Elamites during the 2nd millennium B.C., including seals and pottery, have been found there. Susa, which was pillaged in 640 by Ashurbanipal, then became the center of the Achaemenid Empire with the construction of the palace of Darius I. Colorful images of archers from his personal guard—perfect symbols of the power and grandeur of the Persian leader—covered the walls of his luxurious palace. The immense columns in the audience hall, or apadana, are topped with capitals decorated with bulls, an animal meant to symbolize the power of the king. The development of cities was accompanied by a tremendously refined art. These men, who domesticated wild horses, left behind pieces of bronze harnesses and magnificent figurative friezes.
Antoine Vigne

Tile with images of griffins, Susa, 6th-5th century B.C. glazed brick.

Enameled brick, a technique developed in Mesopotamia, combined a construction material with a decorative function.
Archer from the royal guard, palace of Darius I, Susa, ca. 500 B.C.,

Bit in the shape of an androcephalous monster trampling a deer, Luristan, 8th-7th century B.C., bronze.

Ancient Iranian craftsmen were highly skilled; they decorated objects with fantastic animal designs that are more symbolic than narrative.
Goblet decorated with mythical monsters, northwest Iran, ca. 1200 B.C. electrum.

Camel-drivers, like ship captains, organized gigantic overland caravans, which traveled by ship once they reached the sea. This was how Southern Arabia developed a vast trading network.
Stele of the camel-driver Ldjl, written in Sabaean and decorated with a banquet and a scene of a camel raid. Yemen, ca. 150-250, alabaster.

Many works from Byblos were inspired from Egyptian art, including this breastplate decorated with a falcon, holding a palm tree in his claws, the symbol of Phoenicia.
Egypt-style breastplate decorated with a falcon, Byblos, ca. 1750, gold.

This 12-ton vase was sculpted from a single block of stone quarried from the limestone cliffs near the acropolis of Amathonte.
Large vase from Amathonte, 7th century B. C., limestone.

LEVANT

The Levant, the cradle of civilization inhabited as early as the Paleolithic age, had developed an urban society by the third millennium B.C. Cities such as Byblos were intense trading centers. A palatial civilization developed during the second millennium in Crete and on mainland Greece. The large stone vase discovered on Cyprus, along with several fragments of walls from the top of the Acropolis of Amathonte, are the most visible signs of the existence of an antique site on the southern coast of the island. The large object, mostly buried, was depicted in the drawings of a few early travelers. It was transported to the Louvre in 1865 by the crew of a French warship. This monolith, with a diameter of 3.19 meters, weighs close to 12 tons. Four vertical handles are sculpted at the top of the drum; it sits on proto-Aeolic capitals and inverted palm leaves decorated with bulls sculpted in relief. This motif dates the capitals to the 7th century B.C. As it was designed to contain water, this monument was also probably associated with a fertility cult, under the auspices of the nearby temple of Aphrodite-Hathor-Astarte.
Pierre Aupert

This small Oriental-style pendant decorated with the head of a bearded man with curly hair and huge eyes, was discovered with many other similar pieces in Carthaginian necropolises.
Punic mask, Carthage, ca. 400-300 B. C., colored glass.

This decorative and symbolic motif of a god feeding two animals at once comes from Mesopotamia.
Pyxis (or box) cover representing a goddess, the "mistress of animals", Minet el Beida, ca. 1200-1150 B. C., ivory.

The scenes on this kilim illustrate poems by Nizami, a great 12th-century Persian author. The story of Layla's visit to her spurned lover Majnun is repeated in the four corners.
Kilim with illustrated scenes, Kashan, Iran, later 16th-early 17th century, silk and silver thread.

During the Caliphate of the Umayyad, ivory-workers produced a number of unusually beautiful cylindrical and rectangular boxes, such as this pyxis that belonged to Caliph Abd ar-Rahman III.
Pyxis with the name of al-Mughira, Cordoba, Spain, 968, sculpted and engraved ivory.

During the second half of the 16th century, the potters of Iznik created an impressive number of tiles for the decoration of the great buildings of Constantinople and other cities of the Ottoman Empire.
Tympanum probably from the mosque of Piyale Pasha, Istanbul, ca. 1573, Iznik, ceramic with painted glazed motif.

ISLAM

The Islamic art section, which is part of the Department of Near Eastern Antiquities in the Louvre, contains a certain number of first-class works. The number and quality of the objects—particularly ceramics and metal—provides visitors with a vast overview of Islamic art from its origins to the 19th century and covers a geographical area stretching from Spain to northern India. The exhibition rooms devoted to Islamic art start with a chronological presentation. Visitors see the birth of Islamic art during the first empires created under the Arab conquests, in lands where the artistic legacy was rapidly adapted to the constraints of the new faith. This unity soon broke up and the Moslem civilization developed in different ways depending on the region: from Persia to Turkey, Asia and India. The unique aspect of this section is that objects are displayed in a succession of rooms of different sizes. A geographical or historical map is presented along with the objects so that they can be situated in time and space. Most of the major works in this collection have not been exhibited before, but are now on permanent display to the public. Only the pages of miniatures are rotated, for conservation reasons.
Maguy Charritat

Ancient Iranian potters used the Haft Rang (7 colors) tin-glaze luster ware technique to create delicate effects similar to that of the miniaturists.
Cup with falconer, Kachan, Persia, late 12th-early 13th century, luster ware.

This work illustrates the technical innovations—tin and metallic glazes—and stylized motifs that were characteristic of Abbasid art in the 9th and 10th centuries.
Plate or standard bearer, Iraq or Iran, 10th century, underglaze painting on fritware.

The name by which this famous bowl is known is erroneous: the monumental figures represented on the sides were actually members of the court of the Mameluke sultans of Cairo.
Basin known as the "Baptistery of Saint Louis", Syria or Egypt, late 13th-early 14th century, hammered brass inlaid with silver and gold.

The gilt and enamel technique was developed by Syrian glass-makers in the early 13th century.
Mosque lamp with a lotus-flower and blazon design, Syria, mid-14th century, blown glass, gilt and enamel.

35

EGYPTIAN ANTIQUITIES

The Louvre Egyptian Department—one of the most beautiful collections in the world—was created in three successive phases. The Department itself was formed on May 15, 1826. The initial impetus came from Jean-François Champollion (the man who deciphered the Rosetta Stone), and not, as is generally believed, from Napoleon's expedition to Egypt. Although this Egyptian campaign and the subsequent publications did indeed generate a wild enthusiasm for everything Egyptian—including furniture and an Egyptian revival style—very few objects collected by the expedition made their way back to France. Almost everything, including the famous Rosetta Stone, was confiscated by the English after the surrender of the French in Alexandria in 1801. The first objects were acquired when Champollion convinced the authorities to participate in the first sales of the great private collections formed by Western diplomats living in Egypt. King Charles X refused to purchase the Drovetti collection, which meant that King Charles Felix of Sardinia was able to create an Egyptian Department in the Turin Museum. Charles X then agreed to acquire the Durand collection in 1824 and create a new department in the Louvre with Champollion as its curator. There were conflicts, however, as Champollion was adamantly opposed to the antique—meaning Greek and Roman—motifs planned for the walls and ceilings of the exhibition rooms. This first purchase was soon followed by another, that of the fabulous Salt collection in 1826, and the second Drovetti collection in 1827. Works continued to enter the department all through the nineteenth century with the acquisition of the Mimaut, Clot Bey, Fould, Anastasi and Tyskiewicz collections.

By the mid-nineteenth century, a new method of acquisition appeared: this was the division of finds policy, set up by the Egyptian government, by which objects were shared between Egypt and the country sponsoring an excavation site. This policy continued until Tutankhamen's tomb was discovered in 1922. After this date, the Egyptian government radically cut back on sharing the finds from excavation sites. When this method was first instituted, objects were sent to the Louvre from Auguste Mariette, who was excavating the Serapeum in Memphis. More than 5,000 objects were sent to France, including the famous *Seated Scribe*, the statues of Sekhemka, the jewels discovered in what was probably the tomb of Khaemwaset, and finally, hundreds of steles that were placed in the underground passages in the Serapeum, where the sacred Apis bulls were buried.

All the excavation sites run by the Musée du Louvre and the Institut français d'archéologie orientale in Cairo sent works to the Louvre. These sites included Abu Roash, the necropolis of Edfu, Abydos, Assiut, el-Tod, Medamud and Deir el-Medina. In the twentieth century, bequests and donations brought more works to the Louvre. The Louise, Atherton and Ingebord Curtis bequest in 1938, for example, included the statuettes of Akhenaton and Nefertiti, Raherka and Meresankh, and the stele of Nefertiabet.

The new Department of Egyptian Antiquities was the last phase in the restructuring of the Grand Louvre. Closed for three years, the Department was inaugurated in December of 1997. The exhibition space was increased by more than 50%, from 2,590 square meters to 4,100 square meters. The displays have been completed reorganized and include a thematic layout on the ground floor: agriculture, the Nile, music, literature, temple architecture and mortuary customs. The upper floor is laid out chronologically. It consists of a spacious exhibit that includes the most remarkable works, with more dense areas that form a parallel sequence; these contain documentary series of objects, including scarabs, silex, vases, reliefs, steles and fragments of statues. The unique feature of this department is that it presents both a thematic and historical display, a legacy of Champollion's original design for the department. This organization means that more humble objects from everyday life, as well as religious and funerary works, can be exhibited alongside masterpieces.

Sophie Labbé-Toutée

One of the rare, but sumptuous objects collected by Champollion during his one and only trip to Egypt between 1828 and 1829. This painted relief was removed from a wall of the tomb of King Seti I in the Valley of the Kings.
Relief of Seti I and Hathor, ca. 1303-1290 B.C., painted limestone.

This torso, probably the body of the legendary Nefertiti, is wrapped in a transparent cloth that accentuates the sensuality of the forms.
Torso of a Woman, ca. 1365-1349 C. red quartzite.

Sculptures and bas-reliefs were made primarily for religious and mortuary purposes. The styles followed strict and detailed conventions, which makes them easily identifiable. Created in royal or temple workshops under the vigilant eye of the scribes, they were meant to fulfill a specific spiritual purpose. Yet craftsmen were able to impart grace, beauty, and vitality—as in this graceful bust of an Amarna princess and the torso said to be of Nefertiti. Although the color is now gone, almost all the statues were originally painted, as these works were meant to replace the mummy in the tomb in case it disappeared. Sculptures were also placed inside temples to represent the donor. The bas-reliefs were also painted; these often depicted the kings and gods on the same scale, as the king was considered to be the representative of the gods on earth and would intercede with them in favor of mankind. Placed directly opposite and facing each other, they seem to exclude mere mortals from their exchange.
Sophie Labbé-Toutée

This young girl wears a braid that signifies childhood. She was probably one of the daughters of Akhenaton and Nefertiti. Her features reflect the unique aesthetics of the Amarna period.
Bust of an Amarna Princess, ca. 1365-1349 B.C., limestone.

The statues of King Djedefre, Cheop's successor, were found in the temple next to his pyramid. This head may have sat atop a sphinx.
Head of King Djedefre, Abu Roash, ca. 2620-2500 B.C., red quartzite.

Toiletry items designed to hold perfumes, kohl and the unguents that were needed to combat the drying effects of the sun illustrate the sophisticated lifestyle that developed along the banks of the Nile during the New Kingdom.
Cosmetics spoon, "The Swimmer", ca. 1403-1365 B.C., ivory and wood.

Art did not have the same meaning for the ancient Egyptians as it does for us. Everything produced during this era had a specific role in everyday life, or as elements of funerary furnishings. Indeed, there was no difference between an artist and a craftsman, and in every domain—architecture, sculpture, painting and the decorative arts—each one strove toward perfection, especially if the work was intended for a king or a temple. If designed for a temple, the object had to last for eternity, as did every object used in funerary rituals. Egyptian art, whether it was a reflection of reality or reality itself, was defined in the first two kingdoms; although there was a relative continuity throughout the great dynasties, certain periods did not leave behind a distinctive artistic legacy. Egyptian art did not totally disappear with the Pharaohs, as certain elements survived in Coptic art.
Alain Charron

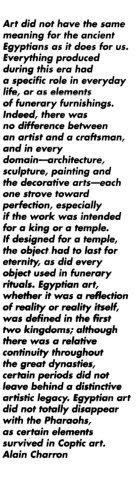

Lenticular-shaped vase, ca. 1347-1337 B.C., glass.

Flanged vase, ca. 1403-1365 B.C., faience.

The statuette of Lady Nay reflects the characteristic elegance and lavish adornment of the New Kingdom.
Lady Nay, ca. 1400 B.C., wood with gold leaf.

Comb decorated with an ibex, ca. 1555-1080 B.C., acacia.

The sarcophagus and the canopic jars that contained the viscera of the embalmed deceased were essential elements of the mortuary furnishings.
Canopic jars, ca. 660-400 B.C., alabaster.

Opposite: Sarcophagus of Chancellor Imeneminet, ca. 700-600 B.C., stuccoed, painted and packed fabric.

Mummification was adopted by the Romans who lived in Egypt, although the funerary masks were replaced with portraits executed in encaustic on wood panels.
Faiyum portrait, AD 30-337, encaustic on wood.

The Book of the Dead, large papyri placed near the deceased, contained hymns to the gods and magical formulae meant to help the deceased overcome the obstacles of the afterlife.
The Nabqed Papyrus, The Funerary Cortege, ca. 1500-1300 B.C.

GREEK, ETRUSCAN AND ROMAN ANTIQUITIES

The Department of Greek, Etruscan and Roman Antiquities, called the "Museum of Antiquities" in 1800, was one of the first sections created in the Louvre. This was a period of renewed interest in the classical period, futhered by the discovery of Herculaneum and Pompeii, and the theories codified by Winckelmann, the apostle of neoclassicism, whose essays strongly influenced the fashions of the period. But this enthusiasn for Antiquity was not new. François I had commissioned Primaticcio to make bronze copies of antique sculptures. Richelieu and Mazarin collected a series of remarkable works when they were in power, including *Diane with the Deer, Venus Genitrix* and *Apollo Citharœdus*. These works, along with the original marbles acquired by Louis XIV for Versailles, formed the core of the museum. Works seized during the Revolution joined the collections later; these included a fragment of the Parthenon frieze confiscated from the comte de Choisel-Gouffier. In 1808 Napoleon purchased the Borghese collection, which brought 400 objects to the museum, including *The Gladiator, Hermaphrodite* and *The Bust of Homer,* along with a group of magnificent Roman sarcophagi.

After the fall of the Empire, the Italian works were returned, but the Department continued to grow slowly with the acquisition of new collections. In 1818, the Tochon collection of 574 objects marked the beginning of the Greek ceramics section, which in 1825 and 1836 acquired the Durand collection of antique vases, considered to be one of the most beautiful in the world. *The Venus de Milo,* a gift from the marquis de Rivière to King Louis XVIII, was a major event, as was the acquisition of fragments of the metope from the Temple of Olympia, a gift from the Greek Republic in thanks for French assistance during the war of independence in 1829.

The Campana collection, donated by Napoleon III in 1862, consisted of, among other objects, nearly 3,500 Greek and Etruscan vases and the *Sarcophagus of the Cerveteri Couple.* Strict legislation enacted in 1870 put an end to major acquisitions. Fortunately, donors were and continue to be generous in offering exceptional works to the Department.

No major renovation work has been carried out since Napoleon III. Thanks to the Grand Louvre project, begun in 1983, the Department of Greek, Etruscan and Roman Antiquities was expanded in late 1997 from 900 square meters to a surface area of 7,140 square meters, with approximately 4,500 objects on display—some 500 works that have been recently acquired or brought from the phenomenal storerooms of the Louvre. In the Denon Wing, the ground floor of the Daru gallery is a majectic passage, 600 square meters in size, that leads to the *Winged Victory of Samothrace.* In this gallery are exhibited ancient sculptures such as the *Borghese Krater* and the *Borghese Gladiator*, along with work from the royal collections and other major historical collections. The upper floor of the Sully Wing contains a 100-square-meter room housing Roman and Greek glass, including some 100 pieces from the 6th to 5th centuries B.C. that have never before been exhibited. Finally, a new area is planned, devoted to the Eastern Mediterranean region during the Roman and Byzantine periods, along with other rooms to house objects from the Department of Greek, Etruscan and Roman Antiquities.

After a series of confiscations and restitutions, acquisitions and losses, bequests and donations, scientific and diplomatic missions and sponsors, the Department of Greek, Etruscan and Roman Antiquities is now one of the best in the world, and plays an essential role in preserving civilizations that disappeared centuries ago.

Jacqueline Monkowicki

The magnificent drapery and movement of the Winged Victory of Samothrace are far from the hieratic stiffness of Archaic female sculptures. This masterpiece of Hellenistic art was made in commemoration of the victory, alongside Rome and Pergamum, over the Syrian King Antiochus III. Page 42: *Winged Victory of Samothrace,* ca. 190 B.C., marble. Below: *Kore from the Sanctuary of Hera, Samos,* ca. 570 B.C., marble.

The composite style of the Apollo, which combines Archaic conventions with realistic elements, remains a mystery.
Apollo of Piombino, Greece, 5th-1st century B.C., bronze.

The geometric shapes of the heads sculpted by Cycladic artists reflect an early appreciation of volume.
Female head, ca. 2700-2400 B.C., marble.

The famous Borghese Gladiator, exhibited in the Louvre since 1808, is a masterful example of Antique culture and is the centerpiece in the new arrangement of the Daru Gallery. Sculpted by Agasia of Ephesus from a block of Pentelican marble, it weighs approximately 12 tons and stands 1.57 meters high. It was found at Nettuno, near Rome, in 1609 by Cardinal Scipion Borghese. Discovered in 17 pieces, the Gladiator was handed over in 1611 to the sculptor Nicolas Cordier, who restored the right arm, which projects along the line of the body. The hand was probably clasping the hilt of a sword. The sculpture has recently been restored: the structure has been reinforced with resin, marble powder was placed in the cracks and cavities, and it was chemically cleaned. Like the Apollo of Piombino, which is a composite style of Archaic convention and realistic elements, the perfection and technical brilliance of the sculpting on the Gladiator makes this an enigmatic work, which has long fascinated artists and princes alike. Jacqueline Monkowicki.

This krater, painted by Euphronius and representing Hercules wrestling with Antaeus, is a characteristic red-figure Attica vase.
Red-figure calyx-krater, ca. 460 B.C., earthenware.

An unrivaled masterpiece of Etruscan art, this smiling couple is united, as they were in life, for an eternal banquet. Sarcophagus of the Cerveteri Couple, late 6th century B.C., painted terracotta.

The Etruscans had readily available minerals and excelled in bronzework; they created a number of whimsical and decorative works. Candelabra decorated with a castanet dancer, early 5th century B.C. bronze.

The rippling muscles of the fighting warrior were produced during the final era of Greek sculptural creation; this classical style fascinated the Romans. The Borghese Gladiator, ca. 100 B.C., marble.

The sculptor brought
the Venus de Milo
to life with the
subtly curving hips,
beautifully rendered
shapes and drapery
that seems to slide
over her thighs.
Aphrodite, known
as *Venus de Milo,*
ca. 100 B.C.,
marble.

The inner frieze of
the Parthenon,
sculpted by Phidias,
is 159 meters long.
It depicts the
procession of young
Athenian girls
bringing new
embroidered peplos
to Athena during
the Panathenaic
celebrations.
Fragment of the
Parthenon frieze,
ca. 440 B.C.,
marble.

Copy of Praxiteles'
masterpiece
(4th century), the
goddess of love turns
her gaze on the
assembled mortals.
Aphrodite, known
as the *Kaufmann
Head,* 2nd century
B.C., marble.

This cup, which was part of the Boscoreale treasure, combines profuse ornamental design with technical brilliance.
Boscoreale Cup, Augustus Accepting the Surrender of the Barbarians, early 1st century B.C., silver.

Pre-Hellenic art, followed by Greek art, became increasingly concerned with a realistic representation of the human form. The Archaic period reflects this long apprenticeship. The classical age, however, sought to achieve an ideal in which harmony was the essence of Beauty. During the Hellenistic period, the turmoil caused by Alexander the Great's conquests was accompanied by the appearance in art of individual emotion. It was in the third century B.C. that the Romans discovered the artistic wealth of the Hellenistic world. They adopted the Greek sculpture as proof of the political might, and in the process, perpetuated the traditions of other artistic forms, such as metalwork and mosaics. By the late second century A.D., the Roman Empire, weakened by endless political crises, expressed its spiritual quest through art.
Corinne Jouys-Barbelin

The new collection of antique Greek and Roman vases are exhibited the recently repainted and restored Grand Cabinet of the king.
Bowl with painted design, Crimea, 2nd-3rd century after C., glass.
Recipient in the shape of a bird, 1st century after C., glass.

The art of mosaic, introduced to Rome in the 2nd century B.C., was soon transformed from a luxury, exotic art to a national, utilitarian one. Indeed, the floors and walls of private villas were covered with mosaics.
Basin mosaic with cupids and dolphins, Roman art, Utica.

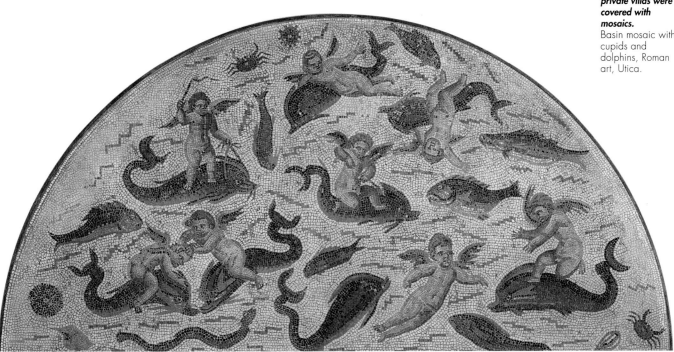

Inspired by the fable told by Apulus in "The Golden Ass", the group of Psyche and Eros was commissionned from Canova by an English collector. But it was Murat who brought it to France in 1801, before finally giving it to Napoleon, a great Canova connaisseur. This work, in which the cold perfection of Neoclassicism meets the heightened emotions of Preromanticism, has been disparaged and admired ever since its creation. With the combination of its anatomical precision and the elegance of its line, Pigalle's "Mercury" assured the artist of his election to the Royal Academy.
Antonio Canova (1757-1822) *Psyche Revived by the Kiss of Eros*, between 1787 and 1793, marble. Jean-Baptiste Pigalle, *Mercury Fastening his Heel Wings*, 1744, marble.

Due to its history, the Louvres' Department of Sculpture, has acquired a particular appearance, reflecting at the same time its royal origins, the tastes of collectors who bequeathed major masterpieces, and the policies of successive curators. Under the Ancien Régime and during a large part of the 19th century, the collection developed under the shadow of antique sculpture. However interest in 16th and 18th century works, which referred back to antique art, soon became acceptable, and for their display, the Angouleme Gallery was opened in the Cour Carrée in 1824. On the other hand, interest in Mediaeval works, with their official "barborous" reputation, had to be imposed by strong personalities. Such was the case with the curator Louis Courajod's donation of *Christ*, which has from then on borne his name. Finally in 1871, an independant department was able to be created, dealing with Mediaeval, Renaissance and Modern sculptures.

What is also striking for the visitor is the preponderance of French art. This pre-eminence is better undestood with the knowledge of the number of masterpieces that the department received from religious monuments (Saint-Denis, Notre-Dame de Paris, Bourges cathedral) and from the Academy's old collections. This penchant is not however exclusive: amongst the foreign schools, Italy stands out, the Louvre sheltering many of its celebrated works, notably from the 15th and 16th century (Quattrocento Florentine sculptures to the Gianbologna's mannerist Mercury).

If the Baroque is little represented – Cavalier Bernin's sculptures aroused no more enthusiasm in France than his architectural projects for the Louvre – we owe to Napoleon's unconditional admiration, for the presence of several famous works by Canova, the greatest exponent of Italian Neoclassicism. Finally, the Louvre possesses works, small in number but of a high quality, from the German and Dutch schools.

At the end of the Middle Ages, and under the Ancien Régime, the sculptor's fundamental role was to glorify the Great of this world through their tombs. In the 14th century, Kings and their families, were no longer satisfied with one single, simple tomb. Their bodies, their hearts, and their entrails all lay in three different sepulchres (as in the Louvre's "Tomb of the Entrails of Charles IV, called the Good, and Jeanne d'Evreux" from Maubuison Abbey).

Gradually the tomb started to reproduce the funeral ceremony itself, with crying friends and family and the catafalque carriers (*Tomb of Philippe Pot* at the end of the 15th century). For artists of the Renaissance, as for those at the beginning of the 12th century, funeral sculptures represented always a major part of their commissions (Pierre Bontemps, Germain Pilon or Barthelemy Prieur are examples of the former, and less well known today, Michel Bourdin, Philippe de Buyster, and Francois Anguier represent the latter); not forgetting Michelangelo's *Slaves*, which was meant to adorn the tomb of Jules II.

From the middle of the 12th century, sculptors were at the service of the Versailles monarchy and the numerous works produced vacillate between the Baroque and the Classical; from works such as Puget's Milo of Crotona, to those of Girardon. At last, beginning to break away from the successive patronage of the Church, the King, and the Great and Good, the artist enjoyed an increasing freedom and individuality, from the 13th century to the around 1840 with the blossoming of romanticism. The sculptor did not hesitate to portray himself (Pigalle's Selfportrait) or his family (Houdon's *Bust of the Artists Wife*). And, whether inspired by Neoclassicism or Romanticism (in sculpture, these boundaries are anyway less clear cut than in other fields), the artist was aiming to inspire emotion and feeling – be it the pain of Julien's *Dying Gladiator*, the lovesick passion in Canova's works, or the wild force of nature in Barye's animal sculptures.

Julio Velasco

This Christ, with an elongated body and eyes closed in death, was meant to be part of a group portraying the Descent from the Cross, in which the Virgin Mary held Christ's already unfastened right arm. This theme is unusual in France, making this work even more valuable. *Descent from the Cross*, known as the *Courajod Christ*, Burgundy, mid-12th century, painted maple.

The slaves sculpted for the tomb of Pope Juluis II were considered to be many things: figures from the provinces subjugated by Pope Julius II, allegories of the liberal arts deprived of a benefactor's patronage, the Pope, and symbols of the soul shackled by its earthly body. Michelangelo Buonarroti, *Slaves: Dying Slave* (left) and *Rebellious Slave* (right), 16th century, unfinished marble.

Although sculpture is a diverse and complex art that uses various materials and techniques, it is nonetheless still linked to the idea of the immediate form, the sculptor who tackles a block of wood or stone to miraculously produce a three-dimensional work of art. Traditionally, the artist first makes a model and then a rough shape before starting the final work. The direct assault on stone is remarkably visible in the unfinished appearance of Michelangelo's Slaves. The Roman sculptor of the Christ, on the other hand, had to assemble five pieces of wood to create the sculpture. Finally, the importance of the finish is evident in the perfect smoothness of the marbles by Canova as well as in the partially effaced color on medieval statues.
Julio Velasco

Images of the Madonna multiplied during the Italian Renaissance. Donatello expressed a new emotion in his portraits, and Pilon, a Mannerism in his sculptures; both contributed to an innovative form of art.
Above: Donato di Niccolo Bardi, known as Donatello, *Virgin and Child*, 15th century, painted terracotta.
Opposite: Germain Pilon, *The Virgin of Pity*, 16th century, painted terracotta.

Decorative sculptures
designed for gardens
appeared in France
in the 16th century.
*The famous Diane
d'Anet is one of the
few remaining works
from this period.*
Attributed to Ponce
Jacquiot, *Diane
Leaning on a Deer,*
known as *Diane
d'Anet,* mid-16th
century, marble
and gilt bronze.

*Commissioned
by Louis XV,
this monumental
sculpture and its
counterpart were
designed for the
pedestals of the
Marly horse-pond.*
Guillaume Coustou,
*Escaping Horse
Held by a Groom,*
1745, marble.

The grace and elegance of this Egyptian wearing a Grecian robe are characteristic of the small terracottas by Clodion, which were popular with European collectors.
Claude Michel, known as Clodion, *Egyptian with a Naos*, late-18th century, terracotta.

When Louis XIV retreated to his chateau at Marly, it was not only to escape the overbearing splendours of Versailles, but also to enjoy the pleasures of a forest filled with game. It was logical that a hunting theme be chosen to decorate the grounds of the chateau, as illustrated by this work.
René Fremin, *Companion of Diana*, 1717, marble.

The success of the official sculptor Pradier was due in part to his sculptures of Bacchante figures spiced up with erotic overtones, inspired by his trips to Rome.
James Pradier, *Satyr and Bacchante*, 1834, marble.

FURNITURE AND OBJETS D'ART

To find a common and coherent thread between a 5th century diptych, a Gobelins tapestry, the Crown Jewels, a Thomas Germain silver service, and a Molitor cabinet, would appear to be the challenge that the Department of Decorative Arts has set itself. The decree made by the National Convention on the 27th July 1793 had stipulated already that, aside from the paintings and sculptures, a home had to be found within the new museum for these few "vases" and "pieces of precious furniture". The difficulty that the Revolution had in co-ordinating these varied pieces under a single concept was to last for the next hundred years, during which time these collections were to be either attached to or mixed in with other departments. It was not until 1893 in fact that the Department of Decorative Arts of the Middle Ages, the Renaissance, and Modern Times (which did not wait for its title before expanding its collection), finally and definitively achieved its autonomy. Nearly a century on it now occupies practically the whole of the first floor of the Sully Pavillon, with two major chronological displays: from the Middle Ages to the Renaissance, and from Louis XIV to Louis-Philippe.

The museum's original collections, for the most part made up of pieces coming from the royal residences (Versailles excepted) and from the depository of the Petits-Augustins, were built up in various ways according to different periods. The treasures saved from Saint-Denis Abbey (handed over in 1793, and partly sold off in 1798) included the King's coronation regalia, and the religious objects and vases bought together by Abbot Sugerius in the 12th century. Acquisitions and donations have served to increase the Mediaeval ensembles, today displayed according to type of material (enamel, ivory...) in the department's glass showcases. The purchase of the Edme-Antoine Durand collection (1768-1835), for example, bought in over five hundred pieces, including stained glass and religious objects such as the *Saint Matthew*

Fragment of a Descent from the Cross, called *Prophet Rothschild*, Paris, third quarter of the 13th century, ivory, donation by Rothschild.

from Grandmont Abbey (see illustration). By selling his collections to the Louvre, the painter Pierre Revoil (1776-1842) brought the first pieces of Mediaeval and Renaissance furniture to the museum: today, alongside those given by the Marquise Visconti, they line rooms regularly hung with tapestries.

The department owes its worldwide renown equally to the range and quality of its pottery from the "Palissy School" (donated by Charles Sauvageot), and especially to its majolicas inherited from the Marquis Campana, which put the Louvre amongst the most prestigious museums in the world in this field. The place accorded to the Middle Ages must not overshadow the department's second section, the "modern" part, encompassing the first half of the 19th century (and in particular illustrated by Froment-Meurice or Sèvres pieces of gold and silver plating as in Queen Marie-Amelie's reticulated chinese tea service). Here again, the Louvre need not be shy about its international standing since it can consider itself to be the worthy successor to the Crown's Furniture Repository (la Garde-Meuble), with notably its collection of hard stone vases being one of the most comprehensive in the world. The regular transfers from the Furniture Repository and the National Furniture Store make up the nucleus of this second section, set up in 1901. There are pieces of furniture, 17th and 18th century bronzes from the palaces of Saint Cloud and the Tuileries, donations from Count Isaac de Camondo, Baron Basile de Schlichting, right up to those by René Grog-Carven in 1973, as well as the gold and silver plating from the David-Weill and Niarchos collections. Here, the atmosphere of the *period room* has been preferred to the isolation and lighting of the glass showcase. The visitor can then meander through the twists and turns of the history of art and style, thanks to certain authentic reconstructions: such a presentation allows for detailed observation all the while recreating the atmosphere of a period or a style. **Laure Murat**

The delicacy of sculpted figures in ivory, the warlike crudeness of a Byzantine relief, the rawness of a Limoges enamel, all these objects have in common a precious quality, which make them real milestones in the history of art.
The Triumphant Emperor, Panel from an imperial diptych, called Barberini Ivory, first half of the 6th century.
Saint Matthew. Arched plaque, engraved brass on a background of champlevé enamel, from Grandmont Abbey, Limoges, 1220-1230.

Painted enamel objects were extremely popular in the 16th century. The portraits by Léonard Limosin are remarkably vibrant and detailed.
Léonard Limosin, *Connétable Anne de Montmorency*, Limoges, 1556, enamel painted on copper and gilt wood.

A masterpiece of Limoges art, this ciborium of chased enamel on copper by the Master Alpais—one of the rare artists whose name is known—prefigured Gothic art.
Ciborium by Alpais, Limoges, ca. 1200, gilt copper and chased enamel.

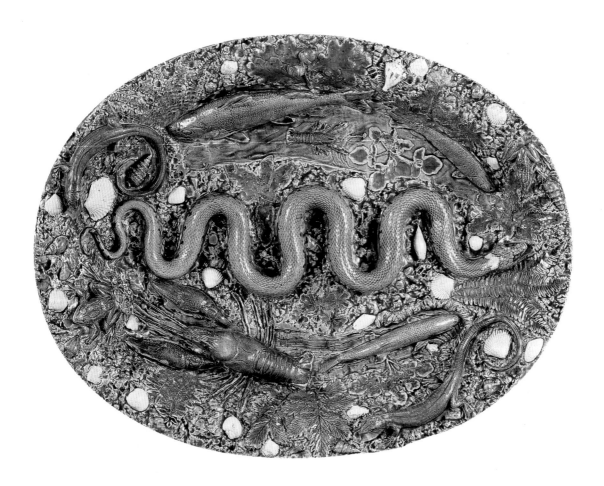

A striking vision of a world teeming with nature, this large dish, adorned with molded snakes, animals and plants, is characteristic of work by Palissy, an inspired chemist and ceramist.
Bernard Palissy, large oval plate, ca. 1560, glazed earthenware.

The Louvre's Department of Objets d'Art—which contains treasures from the Abbey of St. Denis, the Royal Depository and gifts from the most prestigious collections—is one of the leading decorative arts museums in the world. The trials and tribulations that beset its creation, with the problems of categorizing objects that are neither paintings nor drawings, and of deciding where to place sculpture, have in no way blurred the collection's coherence. It remains a perfect representation of the riches that were the glory of France. The exhibition in the Sully Pavilion of the Grand Louvre reflects the spirit of an era and lets visitors examine works that date from the Middles Ages through the reign of Louis-Philippe.
Laure Murat

The so-called "Earthly Paradise", France, ca. 860-870, ivory.

The ewer, made from an antique vase, with a sumptuous 17th-century enamelled gold mount, belonged to Louis XIV's collection. Pierre Delabarre, ewer, 1st century B.C. or A.D., mount ca. 1630, sardonyx and gold enamel.

The crown of Empress Eugénie, the only French crown still in original condition, reflects the splendour of the Second Empire. Alexandre-Gabriel Lemonnier, crown of Empress Eugénie, Paris, 1855, gold, diamonds and emeralds.

Opened in 1997, the Grog Carven Room contains part of the collection of 18th-century French objects d'art that belonged to René Grog, who was married to Madame Carven. Right: Jean Blin de Fontenay and Guy Louis Vernansal, *The Prince's Audience*, 18th century, tapestry. Above: Étienne Levasseur, lower element of a cabinet, Boulle marquetry decorated with a medallion of Louis XIV, 17th century, copper, shell, ebony, lapis-lazuli and bronze.

Designed by the architect Percier, this magnificent jewel cabinet adorned Empress Josephine's bedroom in the Tuileries Palace. Jacob-Desmalter, from a design by Percier and Chaudet, jewel cabinet belonging to Empress Josephine, Paris, 1809, yew-wood and amaranth veneer on an oak frame, mother-of-pearl, gilt bronze.

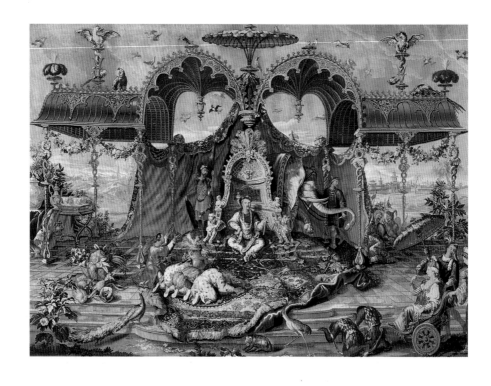

The Napoleon III rooms, designed in 1857-1861, are the only example in Paris of Second Empire interior decoration preserved in its original condition. Napoleon III apartments, small dining room and large reception room, decoration by Hector Lefuel and Laurent-Jan Lausanne.

PAINTING

Amongst the great museums in the world there are few that can boast such a variety of formats, styles, and schools; from Ruben's vast compositions to Vermeers' "The Astronomer", from the Giotto panels to the masterpieces by David, Goya, and Turner.

A richness and diversity which is in accord with the fluctuations in its own history. To begin with there was the will of one man. That of Francois 1st, who generously invited from Italy some of the great masters of contemporary painting, amongst whose number was Leonardo. This first nucleus of works, representative of the formal genius of the Florentine and Roman Cinquecento, was to be swelled in the following century by the masterpieces of the Royal Cabinet of Paintings, assembled by Louis XIV under Colbert's instigation. Thanks to some spectacular acquisitions, the Crown amassed some of the most beautiful examples of the Italian Renaissance – Raphael, Titian, Correggio – as well as a large number of works from the contemporary school – Caravaggio, Le Guido. Also acquired were works from living artists from Poussin to Lorrain, without counting the great historical scenes by Le Brun, the King's First Painter. Finally, as a sign of the times, the Northern School progressively came to the fore with the purchase of works by Holbein, Rembrandt, Rubens, Van Dyck, and the burlesque paintings of Van Lear and Miel.

Louis XV, apart from a handful of Dutch and Flemish paintings, made few acquisitions of old or foreign works, so Louis XVI set about remedying this state of affairs. Encouraged by the Throne, the Surintendancy of the King's Buildings worked for a proper acquisition policy, looking to build up, in a more enlightened manner, a representative collection of the European schools. The Dutch, the Flemish, and the French then entered the collection in force, while the Spanish school, represented by Murillo, made a first appearance.

The nationalisation of the Crown's wealth finally meant, under the Convention, the opening of a museum worthy of its name. Soon to be added to the royal collections, enriched by requisitions of the Church's and emigré's goods, were the artistic spoils of revolutionary and imperial victories in the four corners of Europe. Vivant Denon, its director, structured and completed this collection, consisting for the most part of works acquired as the result of military expeditions. With the same aim in view he decided, in 1811, to collect from Tuscany some of the masterpieces of the first period of Italian painting. After his return, the museum's catalogue included - and still does - the names of Cimabue, Giotto, Fra Angelico, Ghirlandajo, etc. The Flemish Primitives were also much in evidence. Van Eych, Memling, and Van der Weyden aroused much curiosity and admiration.

Greatly denuded by the 1815 restitutions, the Louvre was never quite the same. During the first half of the 19th century, the department entered a period of inactivity, while the Galerie royale du Luxembourg, devoted to living artists, opened its doors on the 24th april, 1818. From then onwards, the history of the painting collections is closely linked to that of Luxembourgs'. The new museum became the supplier of the old: after the death of their creators, works judged worthy of the honour, made their way to the Louvre.

Under the Second Empire the museum had a new lease of life. Art history, now recognised as a distinct discipline, gradually expanded its horizons. And, whilst Giotto and his school inhabited the depths of the past, Watteau and Boucher brought renewed vigour after a long period in the wilderness. Also, the Lacaze bequest made amends for Louis XV's lack of action as a collector. The last third of the 19th century and the beginning of the 20th, saw a rediscovery of a realist trend, exemplified by the Le Nain brothers. A mirror to the fluctuations in interest and taste, the Louvre, now as in the past, carries on filling its gaps, in order to offer a larger and more detailed vision of western painting. *Fabrice Denis*

Boucher, creator of sumptuous mythological scenes, here portrays an intimate family situation in a highly detailed Rococo setting. Its colourful sense of ease, so dear to Doucher, was to earn him the title "The painter of the Graces". Far from this domestic idyl, Delacroix searches deep into the soul by the expression in the orphan's stare and the frankness of the brush strokes.
François Boucher, The Luncheon, canvas, 1739.
Eugène Delacroix, Young Orphan Girl in a Cemetery, canvas, 1824.

After a period of decline linked to the departure of the Pope, the Avignon School had a new lease of life with the arrival of artists from the North. From this renewed stable came one of the masterpieces of the end of the Middle Ages "The Pieta of Avignon".
Enguerrand Quarton, *Pieta of Villeneuve-les-Avignon*, wood, around 1444/66.

jehan rey de faue

The oldest preserved easel painting in the French school, is also the first example known, since Antiquity, of an individual portrait.
Portrait of Jean II the Good, King of France (1319-1364), canvas, around 1360.

To the theme of the cheat, borrowed from Caravaggio, the artist juxtaposes the iconographic tradition of the prodigal son, to signify that all pleasure – women, gambling, wine – is by nature ambiguous and ephemeral.
Georges de La Tour, *The Cheat*, canvas, around 1635.

By the richness and variety of its works, the Louvre's collection of French painting is the most important in the world. Six centuries of artistic creation are there for the discovery. One can see how Gothic art evolved, from the "Portrait of Jean le Bon" to "the Pieta at Avignon", how a new school at Fontainebleau around the Italian masters came into prominence, while at the same time the Kingdom's dignataries were being immortalised by the Clouets.

From the Renaissance we move swiftly to the "great" century to discover the triumph of one master and one doctrine; that of Poussin and Classicism. It is also the triumph of a genre; the historical painting, brilliantly represented by Le Brun. As a reaction to Versailles' hard edge, the 18th century sees a softening in forms and subjects. Scenes of love and courting are fashionable; timeless in Watteau, libertine in Boucher and Fragonard, and sentimental in Greuze.

With the Revolution, the school switches tone. A deep aspiration for ideals heralds a more heroic art; that of David. Soon, however, the taste for the "antique" and the following of set rules in painting is replaced by a greater freedom of expression. Ingres and Delacroix show how to separate line from colour. This debate on form versus colour, between classicists and romantics, dominates the school for a quarter of a century, until the 1848 revolution ushers in new trends.
Fabrice Denis

The first major Nude in French painting, this work brings together Christian and Antique myths: by opening the vase which held the vices prisoner, Pandora, like Eve, spread evil over the earth.
Jean Cousin, *Eva Prima Pandora*, canvas, around 1550.

Parallel to historical painting, the art of the portrait really blossomed under the Renaissance. The portrayal of P. Quthe demonstrates the high quality of the School in this field. Also evident is the Italianate influence in the model's position and in the curtain that frames the composition.
François Clouet, *Portrait of the Apothecary Pierre Quthe*, canvas, 1652.

Vouet's return to Italy in 1627 marks the end of Mannerism in France as well as the triumph of a lighter, more sensual use of colour, inherited from Venice. However it is in Rome, not in France, that the notion of Classicism is developed in 17th century French painting with Poussin. From the same period, and in reference to Claude, came the definition of the historical landscape, based on an idealised recreation of nature through fables and history. Finally, running against the idealism of the time, there is the notable persistance of a more realistic trend, at the forefront of which were the brothers Le Nain.

Louis Le Nain, *The Peasant Family*, canvas, around 1640-45.
Claude Gellée, called Le Lorrain, *Cleopatra's Arrival at Tarsus*, canvas, 1642-43.
Nicolas Poussin, *The Inspiration of the Poet*, canvas, around 1630. Simon Vouet, *Allegory of Riches*, canvas, around 1630-35.

By the choice of a
static composition,
Le Brun proposes in
his portrait of
"Chancellor
Séguier" a solution
to the problem of
equestrian portraits.
Charles Le Brun
*Portrait of Chancellor
Séguier*, canvas,
around 1655-57.

Although inspired by nordic models, "The Ray" nonetheless is distinctive in its greater technical freedom, and its more natural composition of elements, going against the picturesque nature of the great baroque compositions.
Jean Siméon Chardin, The Ray, canvas, 1728.

Watteau was completely fascinated by the characters of Comedia dell'Arte. His "Pierrot" is undoubtedly the most poetic expression of his inspiration from the theatre.
Antoine Watteau, *Pierrot*, canvas, 1718-20.

In accordance with the type of subject matter, David abandoned his traditional models - Poussin and Antiquity - for his large canvas of "The Coronation", firmly rooted in everyday reality.
David, *Coronation of the Emperor Napoleon and Crowning of Josephine*, canvas, 1807, detail.

"The Bather of Valpinçon" synthesizes the essence of the painter's art. An art where the harmony of line is in perfect accord with the most subtle blending of colour.
Ingres, *The Bather of Valpinçon*, canvas, 1808.

Exhibited in the 1822 Salon, Delacroix, "Dante and Virgil" caused a scandal, whilst youthful hearts saw in it the first seeds of the new romantic school.
Delacroix, *Dante and Virgil*, also called *Dante's Boat*, canvas, 1822.

The landscape occupied an important place in 19th century art: Corot was its most sincere and passionate exponent.
Corot, *Souvenir of Mortefontaine*, canvas, exhibited in the 1864 Salon.

By the purity of colour and the simplicity of composition, the artist demonstrates the power of faith taken to the extreme of martyrdom. Fra Angelico, *The Martyrdom of St. Cosmo and St. Damian*, around 1440, wood.

From the 13th to the 15th
century paintings were
commissioned mainly by
the church, hence the
abundance of religious
subjects. The artists were
therefore preoccupied
with a formal inquiry,
which would eventually
lead to Giotto's
awareness of perspective.
We have to wait until the
mid-15th century to see
mythological, allegorical,
or portrait paintings,
themes linked more to the
rise of the bourgeoisie
than to a rereading of
ancient texts. By the 16th
century the problems of
representation are sorted
out, and artists were
happy to bring their
personal variations to the
two great examples of
Raphael or Leonardo. At
the beginning of this
century religious art
becomes profoundly
human and realistic with
Caravaggio and Carracci,
advocates of an
immediate understanding
of the picture. It is also to
these artists that we owe
the development of the
"genre painting". Parallel
to this, and encouraged
by the papacy and
the princes, the baroque
movement developed,
dealing with ceremony
and grandeur often with
a theatrical flavour.
C. Baudequin

A real portrait or an image of beauty? The changing patterns of light with the juxtaposition of nature and the human body, create an ideal of eternal grace.
Leonardo da Vinci, *La Gioconda*, called Mona Lisa, around 1503, canvas on wood.

Posing an insoluble problem of attribution and iconography for historians, this quietly melancholic painting expresses one of the characteristics of Venetian art: the primacy of colour over line.
Titian or Giorgone? *Concert in the Country*, around 1510, canvas.

By use of off-centre composition and discordant colour tones, the artist accentuates the dramatic intensity of the scene, bathed in a non-realistic light.
Veronese, *The Crucifixion*, around 1555, canvas.

The "Death of the Virgin", revolutionary in its extreme realism, caused a scandal, and its commissioner refused to accept it. It sums up Caravaggio's message, one of making the spiritual widely accessible.
Caravaggio, *Death of the Virgin*, 1605-06, oil on canvas.

In 1582, the Benedictines of San Giorgio Maggiore in Venice called on Veronese to execute a painting representing «The Wedding at Cana» to decorate their new refectory. The recent restoration of this gigantic painting (6.66 x 9.90 m) uncovered early retouches of which the most spectacular concerns the green coat of the steward (to the left), until then coloured dark red.
Right:
Paul Veronese, *The Wedding at Cana*, 1563, oil on canvas.

Below:
Guido Reni, *The
Abduction of Helen,*
1631,
oil on canvas.

DUTCH PAINTING

*The political and religious divisions between Holand's northern and southern provinces led to the separation between the Flemish and Dutch schools at the end of the 16th century. Once independent, Holland developed its own art, helped by an unprecedented economic prosperity, as well as the rise of a new dominant class. Church commissions were rare, as the Reformation was hostile to the pictorial. But to make up for this, the bourgeoisie, now rich and powerful, assumed its role of patron of the arts. The tendency to specialise in the portrait, the landscape, and still life, already evident in the preceding period, was to increase, in complete harmony with the client's tastes, which while fully desirous of material pleasures, were nonetheless appreciative of the spiritual. Rarely has European art produced such a wealth of artists, and such a diversity of genres and styles; from the disturbing and sensual works of a Wtewael to the lyricism of Ruysdael's scenic views, from Frans Hals' surprising experiments with physionomy to the soft serenity of a Vermeer.
Fabrice Denis*

The artist mixes a moral allegory in with this portrayal of the contents of a eucharistic meal – namely bread and wine.
Jan Davidz de Heem, *A Table of Desserts*, 1640, canvas.

Jan van Eyck, *The Virgin of Chancellor Rolin*, around 1435, canvas on wood.

FLEMISH PAINTING

Rubens dominates the Louvre's Flemish collection thanks to his "History of Marie de Medicis", commissioned by the Queen for her Luxembourg palace. Outside of this hagiographic cycle, he is represented by various works; portrait, genre, religious, and mythological paintings, which were either part of the royal collections or 20th century acquisitions. This supreme example of the baroque can not however outshine the collection of primitive works, where all the most important artists have been brought together, with at least one masterpiece from Van Eyck to Memling. The beginnings of the 16th century are also well illustrated with a number of first class works, whilst recent acquisitions have reinforced the previously modest representation of Mannerism within the Louvre. Once again, the Louvre can be considered to be one of the best collections of works outside of the country of origin, less obviously spectacular but more complete and comprehensive than those of its rivals.
J.-C. Baudequin

In his uplifting works, El Greco portrayed the climate of religious passion in contemporary Spain, home of Saint Theresa d'Avila and Saint John of the Cross.
El Greco, *Christ on the Cross adored by two Donors*, around 1585, canvas.

Sure of his talents and proud of his recent successes, the artist, who has kept his student appearance, exhibits one of his drawings.
Luis Melendez, *Portrait of the Artist Holding a Life study*, 1746, canvas.

It is with a great simplicity that Goya, master of blacks and greys, presents this young educated woman.
Francisco Goya, *La Marquisa de la Solana*, canvas.

Left, Bartlomé Esteban Murillo, The Beggar Boy, canvas.

Consisting today of about fifty paintings, Spanish art, although poorly represented in the royal collections, reached its height from 1838 to 1848. Indeed more than four hundred and fifty works were on display in the Louis-Philippe Gallery. However the Spanish Gallery was the King's personal property and was sold in London in 1853. The Louvre remains in possession of only two paintings from this short-lived museum, one of which is the striking "Christ on the Cross" by El Greco, bought in 1908. If this loss to French heritage is to be deplored, the quality of 19th and 20th century acquisitions on the other hand is to be congratulated. The Catalonian primitive artists, following the example of the great masters of the Golden Age, occupy an important place, whilst Melendez is representative of 18th century Spanish painting. Finally the Louvre possesses a magnificent collection of Goya portraits, including the proud "Marquesa de la Solana".
B. Debrabandère-Descamps

The modest yet important collection of German paintings in the Louvre brings together several major works of an often enigmatic character. The softness of the paintings of the 15th century Cologne school is in direct contrast with the strong brush strokes and colours of those by Dürer and Cranach, the two great artists of 16th century Germany. Dated 1593, before the painter's decisive journey to Italy, Dürer's "Self-Portrait" reveals the intriguing personality of this major Renaissance figure. The portraits of Holbein the Younger appear much less tormented, combining a meticulous attention to detail with a surprising capacity for simplifying volumes and forms. The 20th century, which sees the reemergence of the German school, would be notably absent from the museum without Friedrich's "The Dead Tree", a typical work of European romanticism. Laurence Madeline

Cranach the Elder made a speciality of slender Goddesses strolling nude through the German countryside.
Lucas Cranach the Elder, *Venus*, 1529, canvas.

ENGLISH PAINTING

It is only at the beginning of the 18th century that a true school of English painting is born, dominated largely by the portrait, the landscape and genre scene. If Lawrence, Romney, and Reynolds show themselves through their portraits as the natural heirs to Van Dyck and the great European tradition, Gainsborough, on the other hand, reveals a greater sensibility and simplicity in his portraits, framed as they are by the carefully studied tranquil English countryside. The study of nature and atmosphere is in fact the second strong point of this late 19th century and early 20th century school, illustrated by artists such as Constable and Turner, who had a considerable influence on 19th century French landscape painting. The painting of English history, less well known in France, is nonetheless acknowledged with Füssli's large picture of "Lady Macbeth, Sleepwalking", taken from the play by Shakespeare, the painter's main source of inspiration.
Laurence Madeline

With Neoclassicism in full flight, Füssli's paintings bring forth nightmare visions and the fantastical.
Johann Heinrich Füssli, *Lady Macbeth*, Sleepwalking. 1784, canvas.

Somewhat inspired by Boucher's shepherd scenes, Gainsborough however here glorifies high moral standards: conjugal fidelity and the joys of propriety.
Thomas Gainsborough, *Conversation in a Park*, canvas.

Reynold's spontaneous and free approach in this child portrait gives the image of a sketch.
Sir Joshua Reynolds, *Master Hare*, 1788-89, canvas.

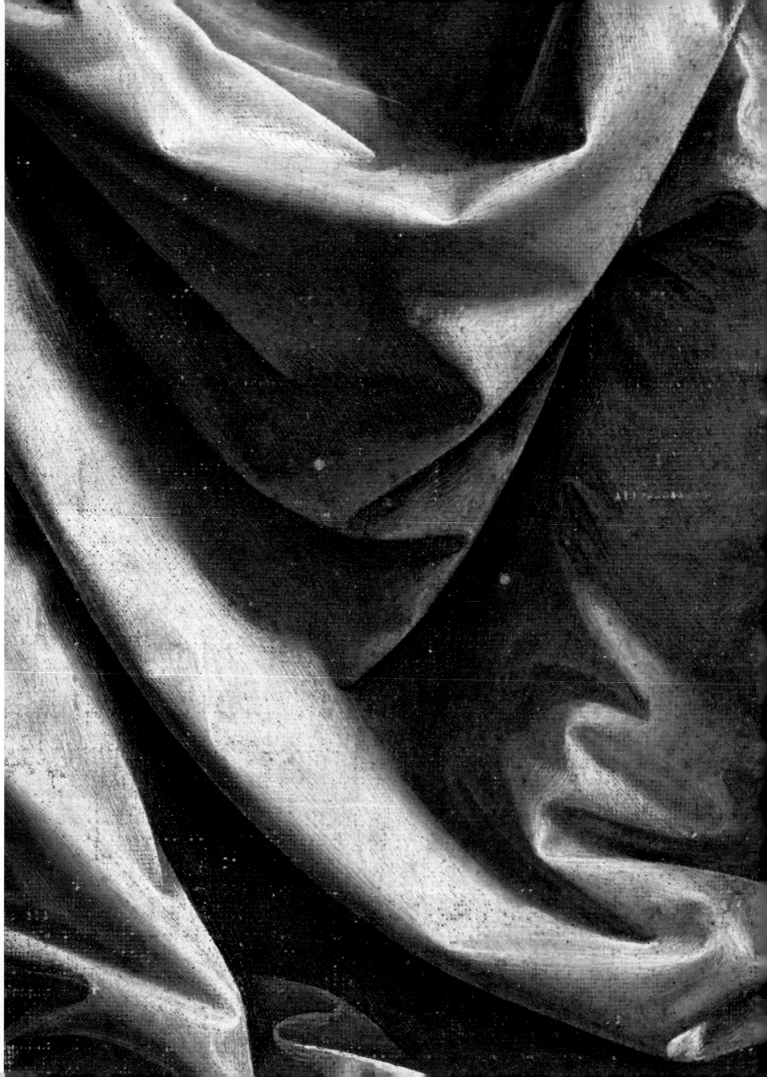

GRAPHIC ARTS

With around 120,000 drawings the Louvre possesses one of the largest and most varied collections of drawings in the world. To be allowed in to consult the works is a great privilege; one of entering into the private world of the great masters. A privilege shared by everyone during the "Cabinet des Dessins" temporary exhibitions.

Painting is a cerebral and calculated art, the fruit of a long process and a developed technique. Drawing is immediate. On a piece of paper the artist has nothing to hide rehind ; hesitations and errors are immediately recorded. In his drawings, the artist is jotting down ideas for a painting, ideas then either abandoned or taken up. Drawings then serve to reveal the artist's personality by unmasking his ambitions and emotions. We are movcd by their fragile quality which has nevertheless managed to travel down through the centuries. What could be more perishable than a piece of paper? Its first hurdle comes at the start of its life. The artist can easily throw it away once having used it. The danger does not stop there. The work gets past from hand to hand, and each crease, each mark, is evidence of its eventful history, until it finds a haven in a museum where the curators will make sure it is not exposed for too long, and avoid unnecessary handlings. Thus preserved, the work can then appear in exhibitions or in publications on an artist or a school, so assuming its function as an object for study. All these reasons, already well understood by Louis XIV, make a collection of drawings as rich as the Louvre's, a priceless tool for scholars, and privileged viewing for amateurs.

The origin of the Drawing Department was the creation, in 1671, of a section reserved for graphic arts in the royal colections, on the occassion of the acquisition of the banker Jabach's collection. There was thus an official recognition of the importance of drawings, which from then on became works worthy of preservation and study. To this purchase was added, by royal decree, the works created under the tutelage of the King's chosen painters – Charles le Brun, Pierre Mignard, and Antoine Coypel. The 18th century did little to enhance this part of the royal collection, but the Revolution brought to the museum collections confiscated from emigrés or from abroad. The 19th century is marked by exceptional acquisitions of Leonardos (Isabelle d'Este), Pisanellos (Codex Vallardi) and Jacopo Bellinis (Album), and large numbers of donations (His de La Salle, 1851-1878; Gatteaux, 1881). It is equally the beginning of the scientific study of the collections, taking the form of a reclassification of the drawings by school or by artist, the publication of catalogues, and exhibitions in the Museum's galleries. Certains connaisseurs, like Etienne Moreau-Nelaton, Isaac de Comondo or Gustave Caillebotte, were more interested in modern art and therefore brought in force into the Louvre works by Corot, Delacroix, and the Impressionists. In 1923, the painter Leon Bonnat divided his collection between his home town, Bayonne, and the Louvre, which recieved drawings by Dürer, Rembrandt, Leonardo, Raphael, and Ingres. In 1934, Baron Chaseriau donated several hundred of his uncles' works. More recently the Drawing Department has once again benefited from important donations: those by Roger-Marx (1980 - Daumier and Delacroix), and Marcou-Trouvelot (1981 - baroque drawings). Although prestigious acquisitions are becoming rare, the Louvre has recently acquired works by Veronese, Raphael, Füssli, Goya, Antonello de Mesine, and by Leonardo.

The Drawing Department has kept its title of 'Louis-quatorzienne', which besides its historical reference, suggests a quiet and selective intimacy. The metal engravings are separated from the drawings, whilst the collection given by Edmond de Rothschild in 1935 (4,500 engravings by Rembrandt, French 18th century masters, German 15th and 16th century masters, and 5,000 drawings) is classified separately. These three groupings of works go to make up the Department of Graphic Arts. ***Jean-Christophe Baudequin***

Preceded by a typical apprenticeship in the Florentine studios of the Quattrocento, these drapery studies were for Leonardo a study in volumes and in variations of light.
Lefthand page: Leonardo da Vinci, Study in Drapery, around 1475, gouache on canvas.
Above: Annibal Carrache, Atlante, 152?, red chalk.
Below: Andrea del Sarto, Frontal View of a Man's Head, 1520, red chalk.

This vibrant study, drawn from a living model (the artist's wife), was reused by Holbein in his 1522 painting the "Madonna of Soleure", the apogee of the German Renaissance.
Hans Holbein the Younger, *Portrait of a Young Woman*, 1522, silver-point.

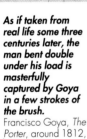

As if taken from real life some three centuries later, the man bent double under his load is masterfully captured by Goya in a few strokes of the brush.
Francisco Goya, *The Porter*, around 1812, brown wash.

The Italian countryside as seen by a man from the North: the detail itself shows the artist's sense of wonder at this vision of nature, and his desire to preserve his image of it.
Albrecht Dürer. The Arco Valley 1495, gouache.

Before being a work of art, source of pleasure for the connaisseur, a drawing is for the artist a phase in his creation, a kind of tool. A quickly taken sketch, a study in detail, or a composition all equally reveal the artist's emotions and ambitions, in essence his personality. Rarely signed, as they were meant for the artist's personal use and hence often destroyed by them, these anonymous drawings can be linked to their author, by pairing them with a painting or other attributed drawings with the same stylistic idiosyncracies. It is important in analysis of a drawing to consider why it was undertaken, but an intellectual approach should not overshadow an appreciation of the sensual qualities inherent in a work of art.
J.-C. Baudequin.

The three self-portraits by Chardin, famous pastels from the 1770s, depict the calm image of the artist at his easel. Jean-Baptiste Siméon Chardin, *Self-Portrait at the Easel*, pastel.

Delacroix drew landscapes and figures directly from life in the notebooks he kept during his trip to Morocco in 1832. They are a vibrant illustration of his passion for North Africa. Eugène Delacroix, *Jewish Bride in Tangiers*, watercolor and lead pencil on beige paper.

Jean-Antoine Watteau often reused his sketches by modifying and combining them in his painting compositions. Jean-Antoine Watteau, *Eight Studies of Heads*, black stone on gray paper, highlighted with white and sanguine chalk.

Court painter Maurice Quentin de La Tour, a master in the art of portraiture, exhibited this masterpiece of transparency at the Salon of 1755. Maurice Quentin de La Tour, *Portrait of the Marquise de Pompadour*, 1755, pastel on gray-blue paper.

PRACTICAL INFORMATION

ADDRESS
Musée du Louvre,
75058 Paris Cedex 01.
Tel. : 01 40 20 50 50.
• Entrance via the Pyramid.
• Direct entrance via the Napoleon Hall
in the Galerie du Carrousel: accessible from
the staircases near the Arc du Carrousel;
99, Rue de Rivoli; the Palais Royal métro
station; and the underground parking
area on the Avenue du Général Lemonnier.
• Entrance for groups and for pass-holders:
Passage Richelieu.

OPENING HOURS
Daily except Tuesday.
Permanent collections: 9 am to 6 pm,
to 9:45 pm on Wednesday (the entire
museum), and Monday (limited rooms only,
ideal for a first visit).
The rooms start to close at 5:30 pm
or 9:30 pm.
The medieval Louvre and the Louvre history
rooms are open from 9 am to 10 pm.
Temporary exhibitions in the Napoleon Hall:
10 am to 10 pm.

Note: Reduced rate after 3 pm
and all day Sunday; the museum
is free the first Sunday of each month.
Advance purchase of tickets is available
by Minitel: 3615 Louvre;
by telephone: 01 49 87 54 54;
and at the FNAC.

INFORMATION
General information: 01 40 20 53 17
Answering machine: 01 40 20 51 51
Minitel: 3615 Louvre
Internet: http://www.louvre.fr
Visitors can obtain information
directly from the reception staff
at the information desk situated
in the center of the Napoleon Hall;
brochures and guides are available,
as well as orientation maps for visitors
with limited mobility.
In addition, television screens
display information on the day's
activities in the museum:
collections open to the public,
auditorium schedule, lectures-visits,
workshops and so on.

LECTURE-VISITS
For individual visitors: purchase tickets
and meet (15 minutes for the start of the
visit) at the Group Reception area
beneath the Pyramid (tel: 01 40 20 52 09).
Lecture-visits are given every day except
Sunday afternoon and Tuesday and
generally last 90 minutes. General tours
are available in French and English.
Specialized tours in French only.
Quarterly programs are available
at the reception desk. For groups who
would like the services of a museum
lecturer, reservations are available by
calling 01 40 20 51 77.
Headsets are available in six languages
at rental counters on the mezzanine level
and at the Richelieu, Sully and Denon
entrances.

WORKSHOPS
Workshops, conducted by art historians or
artists, give participants of all ages (from
4 years old and up) a hands-on approach
to understanding artwork. They generally last
2 to $2^{1/2}$ hours. Information: 01 40 20 52 63.

Above, left to right:
The Napoleon Hall
with the spiral
staircase and open-
piston elevator.

94

GROUPS

Daily except Tuesday, holidays,
the first Sunday of each month
(other Sundays after 1 pm).
Advance reservations required by calling
01 40 20 57 60 (fax: 01 40 20 58 24).
Last-minute reservations are possible,
subject to availability, at the Group
Reception desk. The group leader must
wear a badge provided by the Group
Reception services. He or she may
accompany a maximum of 30 people
(20 for visitors to the Objects d'Art
Department). School groups must have
one leader per 10 students. Visits can be
prepared ahead of time by mail,
by contacting the mediatheque at
01 40 20 52 80.

TEMPORARY EXHIBITS

Nearly a dozen temporary exhibits
are held in different parts of the museum,
including the Napoleon Hall,
under the Pyramid, and in the Richelieu
Wing, the Cour Marly and the
Sully Wing.

Above, left to right:
The Galerie du
Carrousel with the
inverted pyramid in
the background,
and a view of the
auditorium.

AUDITORIUM

Conferences, seminars, concerts and films
are programmed in the 420-seat auditorium.
The schedule is available from the
information desk. Monday to Friday
at 12:30 pm: the Midis du Louvre;
the program is displayed at the entrance
to the room and on video displays.
Information: 01 40 20 51 86. Reservations
for evening concerts: 01 40 20 84 00.

FILM AT THE LOUVRE

Films about art, produced by the Louvre, are
shown daily from 11 am under the Pyramid,
near the information desk (free).

FRIENDS OF THE LOUVRE

The Friends of the Louvre Society
offers subscribers a number of advantages,
including free entrance to the permanent
collections and to the temporary exhibits.
Information: 01 40 20 53 34. A Louvre
student card, available for those under
26 years of age (100 francs per year),
offers numerous advantages.
Information: 01 40 20 51 04.

SERVICES

Visitors will find a post office, currency
exchange services, telephones, wheelchairs
and strollers in the reception areas.

RESTAURANTS AND CAFÉS

- Under the Pyramid: Gastronomic
restaurant "Le Grand Louvre" (entrance
level, open noon to midnight); the Café du
Louvre (entrance level, 9 am to 9:45 pm).
- Mezzanine level: Café Napoleon (10:30 am
to 7 pm) and a cafeteria (11:30 am to 3 pm).
- In the museum: Café Mollien (Denon,
upper level, 9 am to 5 or 8 pm) and the
Café Richelieu (Richelieu, upper floor,
9:30 am to 5:15 or 9 pm); the Café Marly
(8 am to 2 am, through the Cour Napoleon
or the Passage Richelieu, on the Richelieu
Wing side).

LOUVRE CARROUSEL

The Louvre Carrousel is a large underground
area located between the Pyramid
and the Arc de Triomphe du Carrousel.
It includes a large parking area, shops
and reception rooms.

BOOKSHOP

The library of the Louvre is in keeping with the image of the museum that houses it; indeed, it is one of the largest art bookshops in the world. Book-lovers, visitors in a hurry and meticulous scholars will all find what they want in the 500-square-meter store. It includes books about all the various artistic and historical periods exhibited in the museum, as well as reference books about museum sciences and music. It also has an entire section of books about museums around the world, with catalogues of permanent collections and temporary exhibits. In addition, another section is devoted to paperbacks and articles and books about art. Finally, some 200 French and foreign art magazines are available. This main bookshop is linked to different sales counters throughout the museum, some of which are organized according to specific themes. Next to this main bookshop is another shop specializing in art books for children. Louvre Bookshop, Napoleon Hall, entrance level. Open 9:30 am to 9:30 pm; closed Tuesday. Tel: 01 40 20 53 53. A shop on the mezzanine level of the bookshop offers a large selection of reproductions of jewelery, sculpture and other objects in the collections of the French national museums. Open 9:30 am to 7:45 pm; closed Tuesday. Tel: 01 40 20 52 06. Engravings from the Louvre's print collection are on sale on the ground floor, next to the bookshop. Open 9:30 am to 7:45 pm; closed Tuesday. Tel: 01 40 20 59 35.

DISCOVER THE HISTORY OF THE LOUVRE

Close to 100 panels covering the political, architectural and decorative history of the Louvre Palace are placed throughout the rooms of the museum. Since 1190, the Louvre has been the center of a multitude of major political and artistic events in France. The future Queen Margot, for example, celebrated her marriage to Henri de Navarre, the future King Henri IV, in the Salle des Caryatides; much later, Napoleon and Marie-Louise walked 440 meters along the length of the Grande Galerie before getting married in the Salon Carré, which had been transformed into a chapel for the occasion. The major decorative phases and a presentation of certain architectural viewpoints complete this living tour of the History of France. This program was made possible through the generosity of J. P. Morgan.

Panel about the history of The Louvre in the Salle des Caryatides.
© P. Philibert/ Louvre.

PLANS

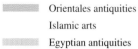
Orientales antiquities

Islamic arts

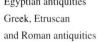
Egyptian antiquities

Greek, Etruscan
and Roman antiquities

Objets d'art

Sculptures

Graphic arts

Paintings

Medieval Louvre

entresol
RICHELIEU

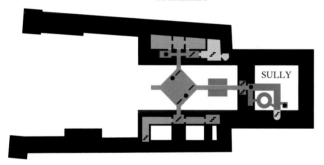

DENON

ground floor
RICHELIEU

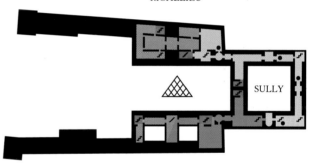

DENON

1st floor
RICHELIEU

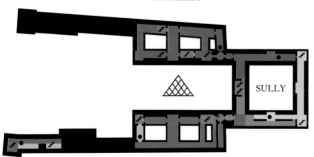

DENON

2nd floor
RICHELIEU

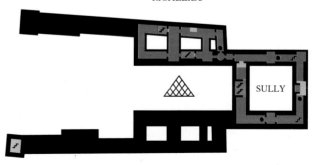

DENON

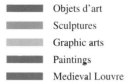

Facade of the
Richelieu Wing on
the Napoleon Hall.

Les Hors Série Beaux Arts magazine
sont édités par Beaux Arts SA.

Président-Directeur général :
Charles-Henri Flammarion.
Directeur de la publication :
Jean-Christophe Delpierre.
Rédacteur en chef :
Fabrice Bousteau.
Rédactrice en chef adjointe :
Caroline Lesage.
Rédacteur graphiste :
Fabrice Crélerot.
Iconographe :
Agnès Cuchet.
Secrétaires de rédaction :
Isabelle Gilloots, Pascal de Floris et Hervé Gibet.
Traductions :
allemand, Karen Rudolf et Mathias Feith;
anglais, Lisa Davidson et Loïs Grjebine;
chinois, Qiao Jing;
espagnol, María Martinez Smith et
Fernando Jumar;
italien, Eva Adam et Emmanuelle Loisel;
japonais, Higashitani Iwahito;
russe, Natacha Iakaitis et Diane Maizel.
Assistante de direction :
Caroline Dubois.

Création et fabrication :
Directeur : Alain Alliez,
assisté de Nathalie Laudat.
Marketing :
Isabelle Canals-Noël.
Tél. : 01 56 54 12 35.
Beaux Arts magazine,
33, avenue du Maine,
75755 Paris, cedex 15.
Tél. : 01 56 54 12 34.
Fax : 01 45 38 30 01.
RCS Paris B 404 332 942.
Commission paritaire 65094.
Dépôt légal : décembre 1997.
Impression : Mariogros S.p.a.
© Beaux Arts S.A.

Crédits photographiques :
© RMN à l'exception de : S. Couturier/Archipress
p. 6, 15, 16, 17, 18-19, 94 et 95;
L. Boegly/Archipress p. 14 et 98; Giraudon p. 7.
Au dos de la couverture : © R. Gaillarde/
Gamma.

Nous remercions SVP TRADUCTIONS
pour sa collaboration aux versions
chinoise, japonaise et russe
et Patricia Mounier du service de presse
du musée du Louvre, ainsi que la photothèque
de la Réunion des musées nationaux
pour l'aide qu'elles ont apportée à cet ouvrage.